CRACK-A-BYE-BABY

CRACK-A-BYE-BABY

SISTAH

In 2017
80's Baby, Baby
Kool 100's & Firecrackers
☠

<u>Reason</u>
No show up
THE FIRST
☠

The Menu

Soul food - Gourmet food for the soul
Spirit control!
Windows- Virus-free
There's a cure for everything.
But it's in God.

☠

God don't care what a person does.
God wants to know WHY? You got to do it .

☠

Spiritual maturity
Faith, prayer, the WORD , worship & praise , you see
Pure fellowship chase with no debate

☠

Faith comes by hearing
No fearing
Testimonial cheering

☠

You can't improve the truth
Evident open love communication booth
Never too busy - Father, Son & Holy Ghost
My ALL MOST / on all coasts
24 Hour power on-line
Mighty Three Fine
Crucial Situations never too grim or dim

It's all in HIM
Ready to dine
Goodness with Glory Shine
A cut above the best
Anytime/Caress!

FOREWARN

CRACK-A-BYE BABY is for the chosen few
Poetic words of wisdom
Only few can chew
Blessed grains of God's potential to children of this land
Part of the Master's Plan
So let's partake for Jesus's sake
The subject is only one
Portion of my divine purpose is done
CRACK is the subject text
To pass knowledge to the next
Anointed advice from all ends
From: ignorance amend
To: mind elevation transcend
No need to pretend
Let's comprehend
I couldn't miss doing God's best is put to the test
Number one rule is to use truth as the tool
To teach & to reach

☠

Deal with the real
Discussin' it , not cussin' it
Time to take a stand
Ultimate understand & reprimand
Take a journey with me to this dizzy land

Defense & offense angles of attack
God got my back
Attest & address with no contest
Addicted & afflicted
Commissioned to submission
To elevate one must eliminate
Advocate to illuminate
To be aware with affection
Beware infection by fatal injection
Ready for the chosen few to chew & digest
Because I've been affected & arrested with LOVE

FOREWORD

These words of wisdom
Keep close to your heart
Be wise with no disguise
Be on top
Don't depart
The roads are many
Only one path
The Bible is the start
To give true direction
With a divine revelation
When you open it
Family reunion
Study communion
Sit & be still
Think & feel
You open the mouth of GOD.

Chapter I

Crack down series:
CRACK DOWN CRACK TOWN

- *The Cycle*
- *The Mindblower*
- *The Kiss*
- *The Sting*
- *The Pipe*
- *The Aftermath*
- *The Advantage*
- *The Panic*

CRACK DOWN CRACK TOWN
The Cycle: Part One

The cycle of life moves on

Menstrual time again

P.M.S. is saying hello

I'm telling it farewell

P.M.S. Camp & cramps a way of life

Forget about it

Microwave beeped

Children about to eat

This man & I - time to meet

☠

Go to the main room

Comfort my man

Hubby of twelve years

Just made thirty-two

Lucky though

Wild rat race in Detroit

Government subsidized commodity surplus

Cheese ain't the issue

Tears & a box of tissue

Say crack instead of cheese & see who smiles

Can you trust your own smile?

Cracks or quacks trying to get us all

Cornered in the crevice like a rat with no exit

☠

Have to be strong
When everything wrong
By faith surrender to Jesus
Everything is going to be all right
I just know it
With all HIS MIGHTY MIGHT.

CRACK DOWN CRACK TOWN
The Mindblower: Part Two

A mindblower
Blew my mind
It blew everything except my soul
☠
I asked for it
Personal gratification without supreme satisfaction
Asking for what you think you need
Not knowing, for what you ask for
You really don't need to cure the seed
Crack affects
Looking back
I'm glad thru the sad
Experiencing life's test
Falling flesh / taste fest
Thinking that I learned my lesson
Interference with my blessing
Falling again, again & again
Stop before it begin
Death is the wages of sin
Rebuke the serpent's charm
Saved by graced arms
No harm

Meek & humble alarm
Falling / Landing
Not in the pit
Tired of my knees
Time to rise with a new plan
&
A new spirit man
Dying from the coca plant
Don't say, you can't
My deed is to plead to be free
Rise from the dead on Easter Day!
Sing a new song today
Body is clean / Remove from the drug scene
Time for soul to be loyal
Pro-choice to rejoice

CRACK DOWN CRACK TOWN
The Kiss: Part Three

A delicate kiss

My husband off work

It's pay day

Close to five bills

Welfare payment to the dopeman

So he can live fair

Off my fare

☠

I'm hit

While I think about next week's expenses

Food to feed my babies

Easter clothes

Utility bills

Transporting the kids to school

Without transportation

☠

The Trilogy: went to work, cashed the check & 99% was the dopeman's

HOW MUCH WAS THE LORD'S?

CRACK DOWN CRACK TOWN
The Sting: Part Four

Children lack

Academics slack

Understand crack

Street-wise advertise

Tearing down the marriage wall

Sixteen years is the call

Dumbly feeling a numbness

Circumcise my heart to know

Once overflow

Love sow & show

Bursting rays of love from above

Now the rays sting & crack cling

Blessing made a detour into Satan's grasp

Change this tall tale

Pious lies

Felonious ties

Conceited deceit

Allergic iommorality

Prime candidate

Gross indecency slate

Prayer & fasting can help the sting

Get in touch with the King

Thank my Lord Jesus again
Moneys gone to the danger zone
Heresy currency
Paper-titled hubby came to his house which isn't a home anymore
What's in store- to even the score
I can't sing because of the sting
Hurt again
Same old sin / Rescind
Blessed with comfort from a friend
Man's heart is still beating
Potential cheating
I didn't have to work Friday
So, I wasn't late on this date
Thanks you Jesus

☠

On time again
Sing about the sting
Crack is not the king

☠

Made it to a friend's home-going service
God bless a miracle at rest
I wore a mask / no small task

CRACK DOWN CRACK TOWN
The Pipe : Part Five

First of all,

Make a call to purchase a eight-ball

Pure deny

Cover the lie

Soul & nervous confusion

Pleasure illusion

Perplex & complex reaction

Safe sex on vacation selection

Devil's workshop satisfaction

Marathon of venereal diseases

Leader in lustful pleases teases

Sick quick

A.I.D.S epidemic

Plague me

Are you free?

☠

Secondly,

Crack syndrome

Faith ain't home

Feel like you nutted

With an internal orgasm

All in your dumb-founded mind
Need to whip your behind
Dictate & investigate
Player hate my mate

☠

Thirdly,
Once you start
Will God depart?
I pray to God
That you don't enter DEATH
Before you return with your breath
Discovery needs recovery

☠

Light my torch!
Arrived to the Labor Force
Celebrate & emancipate
Fifteen minutes late
Precious time constipate
No need for debate
Let's set the record straight
My Lord Jesus on time again
Time to put that crack pipe down
Corner that menace
Turn that frown upside-down
Put in check
Situation complex
No Hype !
One Type !
The Pipe!

CRACK DOWN CRACK TOWN
The Aftermath : Part Six

I put an ad in the Metro Trading Times

My white dog house is for sale

Loving emotional tuirmoil is the bail

Bury the dog house with his skeletal bones

Satan's clone left God alone

Kitty cat loan on credit

But first, he must attend to his addictive habit

Interest worth of non-refundable debits

No wonder to ponder over yonder

Spiritual cripple united to simple

No Crime

Smoking up time

No contempt for the law

Smoke thru a straw

No attempt to correct the flaw

He owe the bank

Need to be spanked

Bloody money

Call me honey

No ease

Spend it as you please

No expiration date on the lease

This is no tease

☠

After holy-hell fussing

The deep discussion

One condition with your out-dated tradition

Time for mind renewal in mint condition

Solution to the pollution

My new edition promised to hurt me no more

Stay away from that crack house door

Crack cease

Stop hurt increase

Before I call the police

☠

The aftermath after the deep discussion Detroit time

Remove the grime & slime

Crank the love bank

Turn one life around

Don't be a clown

Put that drug down

Tradition break for Jesus sake

CRACK DOWN CRACK TOWN
The Advantage : Part Seven

I know the tell-tale signs of being cracked up
Visited & journeyed there
Survived
Know what it is like
Remembered
Listen to me
I know
I care
He can help you
Jesus
Cross dissolves my burdens
I am free
Saved
No slave
Weakness overbear
The good within
Repent for not one or two
More than a few
Countless sins
Therapy begin
Transgress requires progress
Without recess

Plead for intercede

Rearrange for positive change

☠

The advantage

To salvage the damage

Transgressions far from the east as to the west

Strike the high life with knowledge

No prerequisite of going to college

Just repent

God sent

My God is the best with no contest.

CRACK DOWN CRACK TOWN
The Panic: Part Eight

Push the panic button

Torpedoed bricks in the bedroom windows

Panic button triggered & fired

Set me off

Going in a frenzy

Free fear delivery

Captive bound misery

No prep

Unstable steps

Like the virgins with no oil

Prepare to toil

Mind is spoiled

Wear the whole armor

Slipping & dipping

Gibber & fibber

Calling & falling

Filthy & guilty

Lift it

Justify shifty

Like I robbed someone

I have

Break the generational curse

22

Put some money in your purse

God asks for a tenth

Devil takes all what the Lord has sent

But you allow / so shallow

Pill hard to swallow

☠

Stop your clock

Battle with the rock

Worse than poor

Can't rock up no more

No Need to cocaine feed

No want to haunt

No desire to perspire & conspire

Change of heart is the start

The Lord is your Rock

Jesus is my rehab – shock

Prescription in stock

He showed & proved

Always with love

He will move to his groove

Cant fail with Him

Report life support

My ladder to success

I just need Him

Caress / no stress / mainline address

Bless !

☠

With pleasure beyond measure

No treasure
Satan leave you hanging out on a limb
To low to go / flow with the blow
Too slow to know
Take heed to super-speed
Pitty pot want a jello shot
Repress the stress
Careless
No return casino slots
Provoked strokes
Unnatural blood clots
Hypertension suspension
Fly so high
To die ?
Suddenly goodbye

☠

Give highest thanks
Take God to the bank
Now, I know
To panic is satanic
Everyday proud to say
Fight the good fight
God's inherited might
No blight
Only hope: lost child in sight

Chapter II

Crack fire volts
Need
God's Lightning bolts

- *To be True Long Overdue*

- *Zippety Zoom Headed Doom*

- *Forlorn Sojourn*
Three days & Four Nights & One Saturday Morn

- *Satan's Device to Entice your Vice*
God's Advice with Means to Intercede

- *The Isolation Booth*
Time for Improved Truth

- *No Word Spoken Love Token*

- *Flashback of Life*
I am the Wife…

- *Look to the Right*
Hook to His Might

- *Oh! Soul Out Cold*
The Last Bold Episode

- *Missing-In-Action Three Day Story &*
You Want To See Glory

- *The Detour Trip Back to the Highest*
You Can't Buy It

To be True Long Overdue

At this precious moment
It's time for atonement
You can change your course
By placing God first
I'm talking to you, baby
Because you do what you do & you don't even have a clue
Crack chasing, pacing & racing
Wearing different faces
Watch your space
God's on your case
To be true long overdue
☠
Time out for sinning
Stop all that grinning
Sweet begin to sour sin
In these last days & hour
No will power
Need an overdose of Jesus' shower
The Lord is my Shepherd & I shall not want
And you want a crack hit
Can't stop it
I got five on it
We can split
Or else have an unnatural born fit

Progressive evil sin is a dead-end
The nerve to be out cold & bold
After the dose
Play me close
Satan's device to steal, kill & destroy
Messing with crack ain't a toy
From clarify to nullify
Sell-out on grace
Love erase
Descendant of lies coincide & collide
Can't look you in the face
Pure disgrace to God's race
Crack chasing, pacing & racing
Wearing different faces
Watch your space
God's on your case
To be true long overdue

☠

But what happened?
God was in the beginning before the beginning had a beginning
To begin without sin
You have to rightly know where to begin & end
Our hearts are all the same
Adoring & honoring the heavenly Father in Jesus name
The only claim to fame
In the garden, Adam & Eve winning, grinning & no sinning
Then disobedience to God
The First Sin / Death Begin

Disconnected from their True Source

Destiny off course

Purpose too late for remorse

But Grace can conquer the fall of man

Receive pure relief & conceive belief

It's all in God for God by God to us

Long suffer endure for the cure so pure

Just trust

Walk by faith – you must

Get connected to see God's glory

Put an end to this crack-a-bye story

Crack chasing , pacing & racing

Wearing different faces

Watch your space

God's on your case

To be true long overdue

Zippety Zoom Headed Doom

You have to deep down realize inside
Before you can put that monster aside
You - the creation of God gone berserk
When you're zippety zoom headed doom
☠
You can hide & run with the shadow of your life
But, it will catch up with you
If you have me as your lawfully wedded wife
I walk with a wide stride
My mouth gets big time wide
My spirit yearns to express writing on distress
I must confess when our lives in a gigantic mess
Procession for intercession possession
I'm on the Lord's side
His truth, I must abide
When you're zippety zoom headed doom
☠
Credit card fraud investigations without delay
Called me today
I didn't blow the whistle
The addict man stole his own card
I gave my man due respect
They didn't detect
They have it documented down

No need to frown like a clown
Times you received to deceive
Times machine declined & reclined
Where did you go to get some more dough?
No hunch about the keys you punch
New credit card in seven to ten days
When you're zippety zoom headed doom

☠

How to go with the devil's flow?
Where you been in dope head sin?
Do you care hitchhiked to despair?
What are you going to do?
When you're zippety zoom headed doom

☠

Time for that monster to die
Killing you softly with a pleasurable counterfeit lie
Your brains he will fry
Time to testify before you die
The monster deceives & destroys your soul
Time to let Jesus take total control
Call on your Savior to get rid of that sinful & lustful behavior
Jesus' bosom has awesome room
No more Gloom!
Boom!
Zoom!
Succumb!
No Zippety Zoom!
No Headed Doom!
Jesus the Christ In The Room!

Forlorn Sojourn
Three Days & Four Nights & One Saturday Morning

The Saturday

Telephone rings around twelve-thirty a.m.

Prayed for call been answered

Moma, it's for you

It's daddy

Hello

It's daddy

I've been carjacked

Pick me up in front of the funeral home on the boulevard

Did you lose the car to the dopeman?

Hurried off to pick him up

Non-operable windshield wipers & it's raining outside

God's sight arrived to pick him up

He went to the telephone booth to call the man up

To find about the destiny of his fresh automobile

Which he lent out to his man's top dog to pick up his girl

&

He'll be back in a half-hour

But

He & his right-hand dog didn't show up until we cased the joint

To get back our ride around four-thirty a.m.

Four days later
Ride on empty
&
I took the wheel
The eye of God.

Satan's Device to Entice your Vice
Gods advice with Means to Intercede

Satan's device to entice your vice with wordly advice

Phony homeys love graveyard money full of baloney

Enter condemned shack to purchase sweet smack

Need a nose bleed

Trees with no seeds

Zero hero holding prime sacks & slim shady shake packs

Crave the grave acting brave

To vomit is the chronic - so ironic

Discover the undercover lover

Crack attack stand back!

Pills to cope with the bills

Nicotine & caffeine on the scene

Alcoholic drink to think

Lights dimming & wine sipping & sperm swimming & skinny dipping

Dirty books need a look

Lust robust busts

Hunt for a green leaf blunt

A blow to go & want mo'

Teeth as a shark - needle marks

Shooting up varicose veins & membranes

Tooting up insane brain so lame

Magical seeking

Havoc sneaking

Danger peaking

Sin leaking

☠

Five days left the planet

Lifetime family panic

Didn't phone home

Who left who?

Satan left you?

Or, you left you?

All alone in the danger zone

Went out to play, left God away!

Satan's device to entice your vice with wordly advice

☠

Solution to the pollution

Take heed the seed needs the means to intercede indeed

Prayer alert!

This soul is hurt falling rapidly to the dirt

No angelic relic embellish rebellious hellish relish

Mind on vacation you're not well destined to dwell in hell

Be meek not weak

Calling on death - God do not hear sinners

Calling on breath - God hears the just

Jesus is for the redeemed

No need to scheme

Eternal advice to be precise

God's means to intercede

Turn from something

Turn to life

Turn to God
Everyone in agreement say Hallelujah & Give the Son, a nod!
Lesson: No guessing for your blessing/ say with no dismay amen
to the end

The Isolation Booth
Time for Improved Truth

I didn't pray for a man but someone prayed for me
This man, I was chain ganged united to
Related our minds, body & soul linked faithful & true
Lately to date I've shed rivers of tears
With faith, I have no fears
I hate what God hate - the slavery chains within my mate
Keep close to God in spirit & truth
When I deal with my man in the isolation booth

☠

I didn't pray for a man but someone prayed for me
This man, I was as internally, emotionally, spiritually, logically,
affectionately, sexually, passionately with inner & outer expressions of
respected love in all ways one could imagine
Killed me
The isolation booth begin
Skin & sin to my kin became one's secret closed closet closest friend

☠

I didn't pray for a man but someone prayed for me
Spirit to spirit loved the same fairytale dream
Pyramid peaks of love outstanding
Pure, natural & innocent withstanding
Forever & for real no felonious one-time deal
My permissive & God's perfect will

Godly power to use but refuse

But before you ride on pride & skyrocket high to the sky

Remember you were my cream of the crop

My love for you shall never stop

The choice was yours to go to the divorce court

I felt that was the schemers way out

☠

I didn't pray for a man, but God prayed with me

I pray now for the man I am united to because we're

In the isolation booth with no truth

Time to decide never or forever

The isolation booth isn't for me

I need to be free.

No Word Spoken Love Token

Hearts broken
Spirit choking
No words spoken
Love token
Body stroking
Swift as a deer
A.I.D.S fear
Protective raincoat to float my boat
Ready for contact
Love in combat
Moan & groan
Straight faint
Lick where you stick
Fat cat thick
Soul-healing release
Peace at ease
Decided forever over never
No word spoken love token

38

Flashback of Life
I am the Wife...

I am the wife

The wife is the one ... make two become one

The wife is the one ... to be on your mind twenty-four seven

The wife is the one ... desire to chirp back when your souls are apart

The wife is the one ...you share your inner truth with

The wife is the one ... hold & cherish & wear her proudly

The wife is the one ... takes your bull & forgives your shortcomings

The wife is the one ... God loves like His Church

But,

I am the wife ... record holder of the crack blues

- That is my tune
- Married, quite contrary
- Spent more time out of love than in
- While the other half prefers sin
- Doves don't sing
- Tarnished wedding ring world of pain. I acclaim

Flashback of life ...I am still the wife

- Other half ride on crack pride
- Syndrome to the tomb
- Faith ain't home
- Time to get a life

        &

- Comfort your wife ...

Look to the Right
Hook to His Might

High five appointed

Big Three Anointed

I will tell well

Headless male man in denial

No vision is the provision

Mister Crack squeals with skills

Surreal drills

Peace ain't still

Wheel & deal thrills

Still kill

Reveal your steal

Loot for toot

Toot need loot

Fruit loop

Bang,bang,gang bang

Do your own thang

Await eternal jail cell

Real hell isn't swell

☠

A must to be just

When you persist & resist

The length of your strength

You need Jesus' assist

No cheer

Persevere the reserved fear

Fiend'n & jones'n

Mumble jumble fumble tumble

Fist rumble provoke tumble

Fight in sight

A throat choke

No joke for remote coke

I have spoke

When you puff the rough stuff

No protocol booty call

Off the pages all ages

Train loose / ride the caboose

Body sell is the bail

☠

Purified hell

Him & chicks

Him & Rick

Groove slick

Lick till sick

Suck for the buck

Move sly can't deny

Cry

Try

Spiritual lie to reach the nonexistent high

☠

Running from Beulah land

Sinking faster than quicksand

Look to the right
There's your Savior's extended hand
Hook to HIS MIGHT

Oh! Soul Out Cold
The Last Bold Episode

God brought him back

From the dead again

&

I thank HIM HIGHEST

&

Another Merciful Chance

&

I thank HIM Forever & Ever

AMEN

&

Then he did it again…

Missing-In-Action Three Day Story &
You Want To See Glory

Begone! Time gone! Alone!

Life's sampling of gambling

Three days long ago

Didn't even phone or try to get a dial tone

Three days gone

So long!

Big daddy riding a caddy

You're dead wrong

So unique geeked up freak

Floating in the twilight zone

Mister Cool Bones where God's treasures don't belong

Rampage rage

What's there to say?

Wagging home on the fourth day

☠

Here's the scoop

Through the loop

Designer body odor

Fragrant chicken coop

Fashion-sprung dirty clothes

Three-day stale joop

Where's your gold hoop?

Looking pooped

44

Who did you hula hoop?

Where did you lay?

Nothing to say

On what pallet?

Lost your wallet?

And I.D.?

High fee in regards to your soul & me

Did you eat?

Where did you meet?

Who did you greet?

Who took my passenger seat?

So far, the dent in the car isn't the only scar chasing stars

☠

Let's see – to be free

You told me – the learning tree

That you didn't owe the man

Without a doubt

That you didn't owe out

No outstanding debt on credit

Due from your addictive habit

No hurry to worry

Dodging drive-by bullets swifter than a rabbit

So-sorry-sad nerve to be proud led by the wrong cloud

Harnessed to pain

Shackled to cocaine

Unloose them chains

Missing-in-action three day story & you want to see glory

☠

Demons lurking & jerking to & fro

Without a body trying to reproduce its eggs

On my usta-be-special-somebody

Not just anybody

For Satan's sleepless party

So party hardy

After a two-second caress the demons possess

Hiss with a kiss

Diss his time & miss

I have spoken

Promises broken is a small token

Prodigal father who would gather & admire

The crackling cocaine fire for hire

However, so clever

Children & wife for life

Know what to do for him to you

Earnestly pray with no dismay

Demand & command to understand

God is everything they haven't seen yet

More fascinating than a take-off of million jets

But to be mild to a child

My daddy's home with no regrets

No fret

No time to sob, he didn't lose his job

Harnessed to pain

Shackled to cocaine

Unloose them chains

Missing-in-action three-day story & you want to see glory

46

☠

Only a few can chew the food like they should
Let's shout!
There is no way out in a sinner's life but to God
Who isn't a fraud
Let's applaud
Can't improve the glory
The truth in this story
The goodness of life is the glory
God is bigger than everything that's bigger than you
No need to be scared
Boo!
I dare you!
Led by the wrong cloud
No need to be proud
Believe what Jesus said
God is sustaining & keeping
Holy Spirit led – no creeping
You can rest & sleep past sunrise without scandalous surprise
God's prize
Time to arrive & arise
Missing-in-action three-day mourning
Glory made it home on the fourth day story
God's grace is beeping & keeping you
No jive
Alive
To survive without strife
So, you can find your purpose in life past sunrise

Your purpose & potential is everlast
No need for the synthetic blast
Your choice - of course
Dying fast or living past everlasting
Over the brooks
No crooks
Hook & look to salvation
To save our nation
The only way in
Turn without sin
Three days missing-in-action needs satisfaction
Emancipation Proclamation!
No need to worry
Turn to Glory
Moral of this story

The Detour Trip Back to the Highest You Cant Buy It

I can crack you a tail

Or I can crack my side with a tale about crack

Don't crack up

It'll crack your mind

But if you flat out lay it on the line / flat line

I mean if you put truth on the line

What line?

The thin line between love & bait

The baseline?

The base or the line or both?

Is it free or is it base or both?

Make it a homerun!

Please don't shortstop

Better yet

Don't even start

☠

It costs not only in money

It costs your soul

Violating your holy temple

Neglecting your babies

Too rich for my blood

Too high for me

I found HIM /The Highest

When I was underneath the rock / The Highest

I found Him / The Highest

The Genuine Rock / My Lord Jesus Christ / The Highest

My Lord heard me / The Highest

When the world thought everything was so fine & dandy / The Highest

But I didn't / The Highest

Praise my Lord / The Highest

Thank Him again / The Highest

Can't be quiet / Didn't have to buy it!

Chapter lll

Crack Attack Affect
All effect crack affects disinfect…
☠
Character defection need God's reflection
Crack rejection alters Satan's satisfaction
On-line access to God's profusion
Stop all the confusion
Substance abusing / using & losing
Lazar detect under arrest
Guilty at rest
With assist time to resist
Emerge & surge
Paternal & maternal protect
I select to project with respect
A gift with an uplift
I present & represent this present
With His Presence & Essence
AMEN

Crack affects / truthful check / flesh conflict / can't reject / to detect some effects / reality checks / piggy back / no hold back / total defect / no sobriety in society / clarity / rarity / act of charity / effective/ honest perspective / personally, no respective / generation inflammation information/ disenchantment attachment / subconscious detection / crack effect / disinfect / demonic storm / transform out the norm / immoral sin / dysfunctional could-of-beens / behavioral neurological nuts / lower than bums, slums & sluts / multi-mega metamorphosis / escaped God's soulful purposes / panhandle scandal / flapping red flannel / no intense - no candle / remote control/ change your channel / crystal clear percussion for discussion / reality clout / shout out / peace out / cellular beep, peek & peep / candlelight satellite / where are the lost sheep? / simple spiritual cripple / weak sneaks, creeps & freaks / wake up from your deep sleep / homebound leap / harvest reap / reverse the curse / delay the hearse / converse / rehearse/ down & out / low & behind / possess one newness of mind / find & Jesus bind / fine recline/ dissolve slavery chains / no restrain / forget about blame / time to get on the main train / heavenly Father In Jesus Name / ever so clever / never say never / right lever forever / sing Jesus is King / solid as a rock / sustain & maintain sane / mutual bond & private stock / love remain unchanged / ordained / forever remain

☠

(no socio-economic barriers / love carrier)

thru da eyez of sistah

Madness thru gladness

It could be me

It could be you

Grace is with me

It is sufficient

☠

Get the butcher knives & barricade the door with chairs

☠

Over twenty years
Same game
Different players

☠

Went to the grocery store. Bought the groceries. Chicken wings,
shrimps, hotdogs, hamburger & a trunk load of food. Never made it
home.
Groceries in the trunk of the car for four days in the heat wave of
summer. Car broke down. Dropped off at the repair shop. Stench on the
whole block. Groceries in the trunk of the car. Never made it home.

☠

Disillusioned from reality
Gone for three years
Came back like it was yesterday
"What's for breakfast?"
Restless spirit can't rest
Responsibilities of no job was too much like right
A week's worth of changed clothes left unattended
With an overnight bag waitin' for pick-up

☠

(SELECT YOUR OWN TITLES)

1. Beware Over There
2. Over Here Lies Fear
3. Precautions Conscious Conscience

4. Conspicuous Conspiracy of Misery

5. True Tale About a Runaway Male

6. All of the Above Need Love

Going out on the town

No frowns

Everyone's down

Fly hairstyles

Strut your smile

Cabaret style

In a nightclub

My girl with her hub

My mellow:

Pretty as a cinnamon twirl

Easy & greasy

Ocean of mother pearl

Her fellow:

Medium brown shade

Hair of a good grade

Jealous with malice

Then & When

She went out on the dance floor

Cut the rug & swirl to the world

Dancing

Fancy prancing

Glide & Slide

She was glad

&

Flirt alert / uptight not right / he / her husband was mad / so-sad / no fad/

54

Mister mind games / mortal & mental shame / whom to blame in society
with no sobriety / accused his wife with her life / that she gave that man /
whom she was dancing with / not a myth / no goodnight kiss / her phone
number / no hummer / what a bummer in a slumber

Then

She was able

Her mister unstable

Argued with her back at the table

So foul wors'r than a horse in a stable

Went home

Made love

As she slept

Death swept

Love wept

Powers of darkness fight

In flight

Out of sight

All night

Devil's delight

The mister with crack pipe perversion

Sin & Then

She experienced steel pipe vaginal insertion

From him

Genocide / Homicide

How high?

By & bye

Crack-a-bye baby cry

Life's chances are slim & dim

For the both of them

She awoke

Wors'r than a stroke

Steel pipe wiggling & jiggling

In her vaginal cavity

Hells gravity

Went up inside her & out the other

Boom & Zoom

Lock down tomb

Captivity in the bedroom syndrome

While he consume his zoom

Crack pipe sizzle & death giggle

He smoke coke

Choke on the smoke

Stay awoke

Contuse abuse

Slouch on the couch

Slobber mouth sloth

Crack pipe perversion need history reversion

The fatal conversion:

She underwent surgery

No perjury

Six days later / player hater / see ya later alligator

She died under the reconstructive blade

Because he played the crack charade

Sad masquerade

Official monster of a lower grade

Lonely parade

Correct the dormant torment

Be aware of beware

God cares

He has numbered your hairs

I would like to share

Don't drown in the death pool

Truth is the winning tool

When you're out-cold cutting the fool

No dismay

Do what God say …

☠

New age chump for a bump

All heads huddle for the white cloud in the bubble

☠

Five-minute airplane ride with no pilot

☠

Codependent blues

Babies need a new pair of shoes

Heartache & chest pains

Broken heart is sprain

But crack remains

☠

Pure child abuse

Dad & mom that use

Don't suffer the little children with shattered promises & dreams

Because of your cocaine related schemes

☠

Lost everything in six months

House, job, furniture, clothes, truth, shoes, jewelry, car, stereo,
microwave, t.v., cell phone, kids & friends
Now
Gypsy from house to house for the past fifteen years
Living in the wilderness full of fears & tears
Just a baby step to the promised land
Try!
Jesus can stop the cry.

☠

So frizzled after the sizzle
Smoke up Peru if you let them

☠

Wrapped her up in a sheet
stabbed her sixteen times

☠

On top of the world
A bad so 'n so
A man don't want a woman
A woman don't want a man
Chemical warfare going on in your head.

☠

Streetwise with no disguise
Crust for lust
No one to trust
First hit is the all it
Light dimming
Start with a tit
Sperm swimming
End up with the clit

The little dick
Jump on the bones
Lethal zone
☠
Throw in the towel
Blocked bowels
Muscle reflex control gone
Constipated dog-gone
☠
Tried to pry the wedding ring off
While I slept
☠
Jazz me off
Take my stuff
Need handcuffs
☠
A pure twirl & swirl
White cloudy whirlpool bowl
Deep inhale
Heart sails
Ears can't hear
Clouds disappear
Shotgun mouths awaiting for the second hand vomit vapors
Anticipated nervous itch
Unknown pitch
High hitch to a sudden twitch
Personality switch
Secondhand trip

Mind flip

Borderline freeze

Death sneeze

☠

Tap into crap

One-time trap

Snap, crackle & pop

Then you can't stop

☠

Fly home to rescue the food stamps

☠

Mope over dope

Stealing your mama's meat from the deep freezer out the backdoor

To sell for some more

While she comes in the front

☠

One rock

Eighteen months in cell block

Five thousand dollars bond or both

To the point about the joint

☠

Wait a minute

So twisted

I didn't get it

I missed it

☠

One-hundred-yard dash down the street

☠

First & last toke

Smoke the substance coke

Death spoke

Breath took

Final look

Ready for the open book

☠

It stinks

Rethink

Stole & sold hubby's new leather & mink

☠

A mother broke her son's knees with a baseball bat

He deals

She steals & feel for the kill

She got pissed off

He refused to give her the nonprofit rock

Nonstop without payment around the clock

☠

Told them boys

To stop harassing my family

Or

I'll spray your whole block

☠

Twinking

Tripping

Jonesing

☠

Try to find a place to do it

Like you're hiding something

☠

Time escalates
Money deteriorates
Spook is spooking you

☠

Open up the door on the expressway

&

Step out!

☠

Can't locate him to tell him that his momma passed.

☠

I paid your mortgage
I even refueled your yacht
More than a lot

☠

Double standard block
Powder versus the rock
Lesser sentence for sniff up your nose
Than jet stream of coke steam through the glass hose

☠

Living too fast to last
Pushed him out the window
High rolling
Crowd boiling
Horsepower rush
Dreams crushed
Shot him as he plunged three stories down

Death blight

Concrete & body fight

Death on arrival / no survival

No good in the hood

This jungle has a jingle

His mom is single

The hood knew before she

Dead is he

Her son's body is in death passage

Where's the savage soul is the message?

Passersby stumble on sight

Gawk in the night

Celebrate the first day of Kwanza by hitting the pipe

☠

Mention

Tension

Extension

☠

After the hit

Mind is a banana split

So foul

Peep under the paper towel

Thought a hit was under it

Crawling & descending down the wall

Then the playing card on the table calls

☠

Selling stolen goods from a cardboard box in front of your driveway.

(Even a sawed-off shotgun without a box or a case)

☠

From white powder to crumbs

H two O plus baking soda & heat

Presto in minutes

Coke has transformed into the crack menace

☠

Ready for the attack of the adversary

No happy anniversary

☠

What a mess

No holiness

So bad from using drugs that his family would not let him enter their house

They fed him at five o'clock p.m. sharp every day on the porch

Due to thieving stealing activity

No legacy

Once a king baby

Now he possess keys to his people's domain

Now sane

To open the fridge with no revenge to avenge

☠

Low key

It was me.

☠

They take good care of you here

Serve a wet bar around the clock

Ice water on the rocks

64

No dehydration
Five days nonstop
Didn't stop
☠
Take self out of it
Before you take that final hit
Goodness & mercy waiting for you to turn around
Saved by Grace
Holy Spirit homebound
☠
Marvin,.?!
☠
Shoplift you right out your own house
☠
Taxiing it down to track you down
Before all the moneys gone
No scare
Need to be under your Dr.'s care
One spot too hot
Two or three spots
No luck
When your funds gone
Don't give up the truck
☠
I pronounce you & crack
Husband & wife
Till death stops your heart

☠

Give your Queen a surprise birthday party
The king don't show up!

☠

Selling her children's Christmas presents
Shooting up 'caine
Her thang to give her a bang

☠

The question is when to let go
When you can't cry no mo'

☠

Pure dumb
Five-inch shaggy carpet looking for a crack crumb
Found a crack-a-like-look-a-like
Took a hike for a delight
Laid it on the smoker's screen
Fired up - Pucker
Foreign exchange gas sucker
Foggy dew white steam
Made a stinky scream
Couldn't even beam
Scotty wasn't home
The enterprise didn't even land
Crack zone / danger zone

☠

Togetherness
Father & son chilling
Biking, football, video fun

Son goes down the street to play with homebuddy's Christmas treats
While son is away
Father is a dismay
Stole his son's crisp Christmas twenty
To choke on the smoke in the city
What a pity
Left with a crack attack
Monkey on his back
Hasn't come back…

☠

Mama selling her children's only set of bunk beds
Enough is said
Out on the lawn at dawn

☠

Thought you were on top
Sold to the cops

☠

The Fugitive

Urgency

Insurgency

No currency

State of emergency

Need brain surgery

Procedure of contingency / delinquency / diplomacy / democracy

Feel like the little boy whose dog ran away from home & didn't return

Full of concern

State of attack

Matter-of-fact

No collapse

Stand back

Same relapse

☠

Thank God

I didn't get arrested

☠

Fly high / Satan wants you to die

☠

Medicine Man

Young tender with a sugar daddy
Rather be an old man's doll than a young man's slave
It's an all time high when she visits her medicine man
Mister pension ascension
He gives her all the medicine that she can stand
He has to be on his knees & hands
Donkey style buck wild handstand grandstand sex band
Old grand dad
But when the medicine man run out of medicine
He can't do that to her anymore
But just as long as he gives her some more medicine
Old medicine man
Medicine man admits the soul attacks
Possible A.I.D.S. contact
Lustful proposal
Even eat garbage from a waste disposal
Paying for scandalous dues
Peek-a-boo
I'm scared of you, two
Shame on who?
The medicine man or you.

☠

I thought your momma died
The way you looked

When I told you
We ran out

☠

On Tele & Six
Tried to flag me down
So profound / out of bound
Four below chill
Four in the morning
A big deal
A Caucasian female
Her own freewill
Civilian with no pavilion
Frigidly chilling for the synthetic villain

☠

Pure bother
Not my lover or brother
Related to Satan's daughter
No class act
Felonious intact & contact
Pit stop convenience shop
In & out
Get & go
Vaginal sore
Pimp daddy score
Free delivery with adulterated misery

☠

"Robin Hood" in the hood
B & E to steal the stash & the illegal cash

Deal went bad

So sad

One youth dead

Beginning of eternity

His boys said

DIED / DOING WHAT HE LIKED TO DO

☠

Moving violations

Funeral possessions

Honking horns

One-half gallon Seagram's gin

&

A fifth of eighteen hundred

Out the window

Out of raggedy cars

Celebrating death

☠

Gave some love

Showed some love

Gave my daughter's old-time friend a hug today

Wallets missing

She's a junkie

(no friend when it comes to dope)

☠

Stop all the bitching

It's hot in the kitchen

Hotter than grits

Pretty & white for an out-at-sight hit

Haste makes waste

Wait for the waste

Money on the line

Gonna break your spine

☠

White resin & foamed saliva ring

Pus blistered

Charcoal burned lips

Twisted swollen tongue

Shiny face

Can't talk, but sign for more to score for the soar

☠

Elated & inflated eyeballs

Looking through your peephole

Glassy, crossed, tender, popped, magnified, bucked,

cocked & mummified eyed

High beams on / homecoming back for credit for the sixth time

In forty-five minutes

Faster than

Popeye after he eats his spinach

☠

Two drunks in the truck

Chunky & funky

Hydraulic alcoholics

Chuck with luck like the slut with the big ol' butt

Junk in the trunk

Oral rodeo / Consentient f—k

A genital bump

Full of pus lump
After the unprotected hump
Made an appointment with the doc today
What more can I say …
☠

Hershey's chocolate sistah with a fever blister
Don't want to kiss her
Leprosy hypocrisy
Cant resist
Hormones assist
Cutie with a booty
Pure hoochie gives away the loose & unclean coochie
Need a douchie with a double dare
Dread-locked pubic hairs that would scare
Like a forest in the woods deep in the hood
☠

I liked it
That's why I stay away from it
☠

I like it
That's why I can't stay away from it
☠

The Imposter

A cry for help :
Black woman pose as a white woman
To cash the white woman's check
Forgot to look in the mirror
☠
Left us
Love of both worlds
Her & the drug

After Viewing, "My Brother, Marvin"

Say it loud!
Bold strongholds out cold
Alcoholic dad burdened with jealousy & pride
Say it loud!
Bold strongholds out-cold
Cocaine line addicted son burdened with anxiety & frustration
Say it loud!
Bold strongholds out cold
Battle of demonic spirits collide
No defeat conceit & deceit
Wife & mother in the middle abide
Maternal instincts coincide
Dad's spirit of abscess with no success
Says incest
No contest
Shoots his own son dead
Pure detest / no house arrest / free rent / no jail time spent
☠
Dynasty fantasy
Dreams unseen
Fiend so lean
No green
Not clean
Clone a loan

Lost at all costs

☠

On the mission run

Come & get her daughter's social security check fund

I'm glad

Crack buddies mad

I got the cash

Our prerogatives clash

☠

Friend turned into stranger

☠

Hustler / Customer

Ballers / Callers

Calling & falling

First five hundred

I got you

Or

Get Jesus

☠

Understand your position regardless of your condition

As Moses

Let my people go

I have to let him go

☠

Revolving lay-a-way plan for a man or an old school fool at your

disposal

Decent proposal for a garbage disposal

Or

Tart fart head start sweetheart

On the side / not the bride

Feelings collide

Not just your extraordinary A.T.M. good looking no hooking 'ho

Not looking for the dough

Automatic systematic

Sell me out without a thirty-day notice

Like a bounced check

What the heck?

No peck on the cheek

In check

No touch of the volcanic breast

Pumped up chest

No slap on the pyramid ass

Buck raw piece of class & sass

Your lass in the not-so-distant past

Being fast

Six a.m. never lasting everlasting

Lawsuit due

Prosecutor sue

That's your clue!

No sunrise

No surprise

No arise

☠

Laid off from the auto plant

Need money is the chant

Sell it to make a profit

The bills are due

This is true

☠

Before you know

More money

No!

Hold the stash have a big bash

Smoke up your cash

Hiding out

Nervous about

No doubt

Hide & you can't find

The man is looking for you

The clue

When one find whip your behind

Can't even recognize

The man can

Make matters worse to honor the curse

☠

Signifying monkey

Dignified junkie

Outcast lucky

☠

Spooky tools

Loose stools

Death pool

Precarious fool

☠

Home transformed to condemned shack

Light, gas, water & phone disconnect

Fatal consequences intact because of crack

Sick chick

Ready & quick

Have a fatal wick

Clothes hanger wire is the attire

For the butane crackling fire

For the torch that won't scorch

Dip the cotton ball in the alcohol

For a flame you can't tame

Getting high in the dark

Where's the spark

A deadly shark

☠

Down so low

Open the door

Gliding & slithery sliding like a rattlesnake on the floor

Stealing out your peeps coats & pants pockets

Off your rocket

While I sleep

You creep in the deep

☠

Dummy packs!

Wrong sacks!

No true intent

Light bulb contents

White florescent

Crystals sold as cocaine

So lame

Stop blood flow in main vein

Heart attack on contact

Exact fact

Camouflaged combat

Serpent strikes the sheep in disguise

Paranoia on the high rise for the unwise

☠

The electronic bank camera took your picture

Withdrawing your mother-in-law's funds without permission

To the top of the roof

He denied the sinful proof

☠

God didn't put that taste in your mouth

Whom influence your consequence

You did?

God forbid

☠

Since I can't pay

Let's sleep away

Pray

☠

Men speculate pure distaste

Headlock / cock block / deadlock

Woman on a dirty couch

Holding on to the tools & pouch

Doing it to a dog

Dog licks make me sick
Mind in a fog
For a ten-cent rock
Small shock
Rubber gloved dude doing the surgical task

☠

God didn't put that taste in your mouth
Whom influence your consequence?
You did?
God forbid

☠

Since I can't pay
Let's sleep away
Pray

☠

Men speculate pure distaste
Headlock / cock block / deadlock
Woman on a dirty couch
Holding on the to the tools & pouch
Doing it to a dog
Dog licks make me sick
Mind in fog
For a ten-cent rock
Small shock
Rubber gloved dude doing the surgical task
Wearing a doctor's mask
Led the shepherd's rod into her bod
Just for the three seconds blast last

A bloody swatch

Watch!

Stopwatch

A woman on a dirty couch

☠

Two-legged traitor not ready for maker headed to the undertaker

Then: Take a blast & cross my legs

Now: Three ring circus going on & the devil's in the center

☠

Friendly hand waver

Hot in the scorching sun

With winter wool coat & cap

Need a shower

Played organ pipes with his nose

Asked me for money for his honey

Played me almost close

Scratched at his chest

Generational curse at its best

Raw for the raw outlaw

I saw

☠

Burnt toffee

Speedball with coffee

☠

So high homey

Raped & stole her money

From her private cave

How grave

☠

Solicit a man minding his own business
Gold nugget ring for sale
Crack is the unknown bait
Pure gold worth a c-note is sold
Gold ring turned green
Sold gold that was out-cold bold

☠

Vulture
Barbaric culture
Frail tail
Pelican skeleton
Skin & bones jones

☠

Credit card kleptomaniacs
To soothe the crack attacks

☠

Meltdown for the vein / totally insane
Crack crave living in a rat's maze
Time for a raise
Let me amaze
Extinguish the blaze
Time to be brave

☠

Graduate from the trees to the crack house
On the dean's list
Persist to resist
Be sincere

Live without fear

God hears & is here

☠

Drunk

Copping

Hood rat stole seven hundred out my back pocket

☠

Dark spark leave its mark

☠

Safeway to tame

Cure the lame

Claim remains the same

Don't blame

Jesus is the name

☠

No trace

No sign

Slips into darkness

Chain linked in a eye blink

Weak wink

Time to think

Too late you sink

☠

Forlorn porn

Sojourn

Morn torn

The thorn

No corn

☠

Insecure for sure

Thrive to connive

Capture enemy thoughts

Destiny can't be brought

Chasing pipe dreams

Headed down stream

Triple beam glean & gleam

Glaze

Blaze

Craze

Phase

☠

Bike pedal to the metal

Buyer / Seller

Settle to meddle

Goods to peddle

Weighed for the trade

Homemade packs / Custom made sacks

☠

Filing for divorce ran across my mind today

Same replay

Hard thought to erase

Crack is the she

That use-ta be me

☠

Electric slide in tears

Saltwater isn't the only fear

☠

Selling crack off the ice-cream truck

☠

Need a doctor's excuse to save your job
Even though you rob

☠

The demons hitchhike a ride when you use with abuse
Seven spirits abide to your unattached soul for control
State is worst than before
Time for faith in fasting & prayer, evermore

☠

Had to peel his seven–month-old-no-change socks

☠

No surcharge
Hell express – fringe benefit package
It's my birthday
My baby is getting my hair done
Shopping spree at the mall / THAT'S NOT ALL
Cheese wining & candlelight dining
Luxury penthouse suite
Room service & passionate kisses
Jacuzzi & Music
Skinny dip swimming
Whirlpool & jewels
But instead, my baby only got her hair done
Waiting alone
Sidetracked
After the first hit

Residing in the pit
Three days later
Hooked to that S H_T!
☠

Home wreck Christmas bonus check
☠

Memory lane pain
Hang out with folks that use
Everybody lose
☠

Say in Jesus name
&
LIE.
☠

Hold driver's license in hostage
So you can't cash the check
☠

Love is stronger than death
Jesus wept
☠

Expectant mom smokes fifty-ones on a daily basis
Eight months
One month to go
☠

Buck-eyed / cop car sirens / schizoid / psychosis / bionic ears /
sound effects
Got to go!
☠

Big clout

Pig snout

Show out

No doubt

Money stout

Got caught

☠

narrating slobber mouth / deafened audio alert / mute acute aggravating anxiety attacks / must have a drink transformed into must hold the coke bowl / no time to pass it

☠

sell it / semi- sweet / stealing jezebel / somewhat sexy / smiley /spineless / sneaky / snaky / shaky / satiny smooth / stripping sensation / secret slight / sullen skulk / fully sully / sad sulk in bulk / slowpoke like a snail / possessing stylized stunts like pucker up buttercup straw in the mouth blowing / belching profusely the substance then she sails / here comes hell

☠

one of the clan or all of the three stole my stuff & kept visiting the A.T.M. I hope the bank ain't keeping a twenty-four-hour scan / I wonder what the neighbors are thinking / no blinking / nothing is stopping me after the master blast to go as I please / even to run outside / react after the attack

☠

Pocket searcher, regulator, ready freddie, frenzy, frantic, fantastic, fantasized emotional turmoil, heightened horny appetite, sexual promiscuity, lust on the X-rated page rampage & on the loose rage

☠

A tripping thinker

Conscious tinker

Cops are coming!
Motion for commotion
Take cover
Seven feet tall basketball player
Size seventeen tennis shoes
Hides & dives into the closet
Only the pizza man

☠

Don't pay the tab
Selective memory loss
Added to the sauce

☠

My off-duty ace likes outer space
Outhouse smoking bandit
Embark on the sound of the kiss
Can't dismiss
Totally against
Outlawed against shame to blame
Playing with time
Started with a dime
Can't tame the inferno flame

☠

Immediate gratification
No satisfaction

☠

Woe boy
No toy
No monkey business riding my back

A gorilla is the deal
Beaded sweat a popping
Buffalo head a nodding
I have no time to scratch
Get out the mirror picking your face
Prostituting thoughts
Whether mate is faithful or not

☠

Unforgettable past
Scooped maggots from the infected thigh
Threw the maggots on the floor
Shot up
Bandaged the spot
Now
Ten years clean from the drug scene

☠

Didn't eat for six days
Twenty-seven hundred dollars
Nine hundred in the left sock
Nine hundred in the right sock
Nine hundred in the right pocket

☠

All time cure for arthritis
The way she moves them shoulders
Petty pathetic pacifier
Sipping gases like a baby
When the gases stop
The whining starts

Time to be weaned

☠

distasteful & debonair Deceita Devoura constantly constipated with a
feudal case of diarrhea of the mouth proudly puffed out shamelessly &
arrogantly cussing you out in stench surroundings. Need to put a clapper
on this but she passes one bowlful to get five people high on one light.
Nightlife to daylight. With the window shades up in public view, no clue.

☠

I.O.U. from the man
With my name backing credit
News to me
Knew nothing about it

☠

Know where to cop a boulder as big as your shoulder
White flight / pure blight / delight changed into a big fight

☠

Do the heinous or not so heinous crime & do the time
In the sitting cell / sitting still
No faking / no blanket
Feed you frozen peanut butter & jelly sandwiches
But across the line you get "Mickey D's".

☠

Adventure start off the charts
East side / West side / City wide / Nation wide
Airtime voyage / Vintage courage

☠

News before the blues
Sport the "ports" / flick a nick

Decide the bud you desire to choose with the booze

Northern lights / AK-47 / rego / black widow / larry / hog breaths /

purps

Or

Kush

What you do?

When the blunt canoe

Miss the hit / Get with it

Spit on it

Even & slow

Go with the flow…

☠

You's tha woman

She's tha bitch

☠

So-called cool – the main fool

A rock dime to dine on time with just fine

Fine as Boones Farm wine

Drawstring fourteen-inch ponytail / eyelash strips / master stretch pants

From the beauty supply

To sport the loose booty & the beauty

Talking lip & leather whip

Okey dokey before the okey doke

One mo' fo' sho'

Merge for the splurge

Tricky twinkie

Stop thinking

Time ticking

Crime blinking & Titanic sinking

☠

Bury past with brand new mercy

God didn't let your sin cancel your purpose in life

☠

Forget-you

Wish he would

The "G" in the hood

Civilized yet wise

Sophisticated not fornicated

Debonair with no hair

Strap over that

Forget -you

Hater girl

Hater girl

Why you look so grim

Lost gem

Need a dose of Kem

It's not that dim

Ask & it shall be given

I know

FORGAVE

The forgiven forgiveness

Forget-you-not

No lure

No perjure

For sure

☠

Synthetic pee or niacin to get the job

☠

Run-a-way bride hasn't seen hubby in 2 weeks

☠

Maker shake -up before the take up

Wake up for the earthquake

For HIS SAKE

MAKE

all before the roll call

No fake

He take

One who hears his voice

Do his will by choice

☠

Sneak peek at the freaks

Can't sleep all week

☠

Squatter will squat at a vacant lot – any spot

☠

No frills

The thrill kills before God get the news

☠

Internet access

Cyber-sex excess

Explore

Deplore deploy

Enjoy

No recess

Reborn

Abnorm porn

In the early morn

No time to sojourn

Chat room chat lead to cyber seduction

Text

Next

Then we meet in the sheets with the out-cold stones to float our boats

Boast before the roast

Honorary participants time to toast

The invisible demonic ghost

☠

Help is on the way

Mark my words to what I say

☠

Devasto Disasterly destined in diverse &

perverse directions deceiving with

defensive mechanisms of spiritual warfare always

enticing instigations not

worth investigation / main conspirator constipating conspiring

controversial conceptions while consuming the crippling crutch

☠

Off the cliff

Brain signal shift

You don't need a dance partner

Waltz on

Hustle gone

Piece of lint

Bread crumb
Looking on the floor
For the non-existent
White
Microscopic piece

☠

Super faced
Swift shoplift
Superficial insignificant
Seven-folded secrets
About a real reliable source
That isn't reliable anymore
Searching for the unsearchable reason
While freeze drying one's brain cells

☠

No riot
Hush Be Quiet will raise havoc with hell
Always blaming someone else
When her life's not swell
Will holler for the almighty dollar
Life's tunnel vision need revision
Her decisions
Right eye see the dollar
Left eye see the rock

☠

Get your razor blade & plate ready
Self-service station serving suicide

Cleverly cunning in the catalytic state of catastrophic confusion

☠

Base Rental

Out of dope

Out of cash

Rent your wheels to the man

Car has a proud new owner

The man

☠

Left my rock pattern

Unattended

After jet lag

Rock pattern has changed

No contest in this conquest

No honesty in this dynasty

☠

Look out crew

Head screws

Window peepers at the same time

Robotic heads never touch

Scatterbrains at the windowpane

☠

Cracker jack snack on smack & crack

☠

Conspire or perspire your desire

Retire from that fire

Feeding fetus a well balanced crack diet
through the umbilical cord passage
Loathe wisdom
Self-abort from the start
Low birth rate is the case
High mortality fate
Crave grave
Withdrawn baby child
Irritably crying
Hollering wild
Ward of the state
Child protective services has a date

☠

It's curable
God is able

☠

Monday to Thursday / at home stay
Friday / payday
Safeway
No way
Go astray
Pure dismay
There's price you pay when you go out to play
Payback tomorrow
All time high
Blackmail to pay for the bail
Lifestyle headed for the jail

☠

Perfumed aura
Smooth gratifying horror
Fast acting drain
Vapor raw pain
Stones catching sparks
Leaves a prophetic mark
Doom & gloom

☠

Yellow like butter
Makes you stutter
Can't even utter
Sound like a mutter

☠

Stalk the thought
If walls could talk
Walk the Christ-like walk
Time out for the talk
You were better taught

☠

Mr. Mom taking care of the home front
Wife worked the afternoon shift
Left his two tots unattended in the bathtub
While he stepped out for a zoom
Living room / dining room / kid's bedroom set
Traveled out the backdoor
In payment for crack rock score
Wife came home at the end of her shift
Kids are still in the tub

Where's her hub?

☠

Not a saint

So irate

On the scene

That man is mean

Stole & grabbed my stones

At gunpoint

Smoked them in front of my face

Not my ace

☠

Knock on the door

Lie & say he's not there

But he's there

Who's scared?

☠

Monster transformation for your information

☠

Far cry from joy

Can't deny

When you scope out your synthetic homeboy out on the loose

Forgot about his job, family & papoose

Out on the deep end

Doing drug abuse

Tough luck

It sucks

Wasting bucks

Wife at end of her caboose

She's mad far from glad

Making divorce operations / bank transactions

To keep money from the strange man in the land

☠

Cruising the hood with her homegirl's new Denali

Enjoy the moment before the torment

Glanced at the side mirror to the rear

Do you hear?

In the daylight

"Pullover to the right!"

Husband's car pass in sight

Emotions can't register fright

"Whatever it takes, I'll pay! Don't let that car get away."

Reality sail

Denali on the tail

With no debate

A get-a-way car chase

No way to succeed

Neon in the lead

Changing fast lanes

Feeling the pain

Denali to the left

Neon carrier of potential theft

With cry & plead

Denali in the lead

Heart race with a lethal pace

Traffic block / nonstop clock

Neon zooming

Straight ahead
Being misled
Demonic laughter in the air
Crack ain't scared
Church friend on his passenger side
Ready for Satan's fired-up, spaced-out ride
Minus the bride
Crack abide

☠

In September I'll always remember
Jesus care through the despair
Is it fair?
Husband don't care
Time out for Kleenex tissue
Time to resolve critical issues
Depart the broken heart
Straight ahead
Fresh new start

☠

Drugs are calling
Won't even get a haircut
With a thousand buckaroos in your pocket
Food never make it to the freezer
Balloons never make it to the party

☠

War zone
Better ask somebody
Identify territory

☠

Don't answer telephone calls
Treat like a bill collector

☠

A "wet" blunt
Undercover in disguise
Start fighting with the police
A citizen of the law

☠

Closet smoker
No secret like a storm
Cover up within the norm

☠

Old school
One-fourth inch stem
Hooter
Sharpshooter
Nasal tooter
One fifty-one rum
Cotton ball & alcohol
No tame flame
Chore boy ole boy
No toy
Clothes hanger wire dipped for the fire
Can't retire

New school
Use anything with a hole

To withstand the heat

For the fool

(I.E. car antennas, hardware screws)

As the tool

To inhale the crack pulls

Drool

Death pool school

☠

So whack

On her back

Funky splash

Naked flash

Eat it & take all the juices

For the dope to cope

So remote

☠

Stealing copper pipes & rails / aluminum gates / vinyl siding &
chimney lining if you have a ladder & tools from vacated properties
/ that property isn't yours/ / going / gone for dirty thirty & up / more
than a panhandle cup

☠

Eight ball call after the fall

☠

All jokes aside

Her boo friend introduced her to a line & a combination plate

Commemorating her thirtieth birthday on this date

Snort & sniff for the miss

No superimpose

Raw membranes of the nose froze

Alcoholic lush / slush added to the rush

Love chick now two decades sick

No pulpit – the culprit who introduced the abuse

Abused

After what she became

Confused

Everyone lose

☠

Sugar Booger

☠

Home security defense makes sense

Shock the block

Steal / kill & destroy the sweetness out of sugar

&

Steal / kill & destroy the savor flavor out of salt

☠

I met a man who told me his life story in five minutes. Detroit was the
word that rang in his memories. He use-ta work at Dodge Main.

Can't hide forensics

Can't hide D.N.A.

Can't hide the truth

In Atlanta at a homeless shelter, introduced himself with a jigsaw
puzzle of the Big D. His story was not boring. When he got his check
on Thursday night. They knew. He knew. They wouldn't see him till
Monday. Do you know how many crack houses you pass from Twelfth
Street to Mound Road? He let the cabbie hold twenty while he hit a spot.
Time lapsed so he told him to ride out. Lost that job. Went to the dirty

south to find a drug free life. Found a job. Free for two years. But in nineteen ninety-nine met a chick at the strip joint. You just passed. Went to the hotel. She stayed in the bathroom too long. I went on in. I should of called my sponsor but I didn't. The set up was all set up. Upset. Beginning of the worldly journey. Lost that job. End up sleeping under the bridge you just passed. To the rescue at the rescue mission. Blood gonna get a job. Clean drop. Dressed in shirt & tie. Mr. Crack says good-bye …

☠

Who took the damn bike?
Three o'clock a.m.
Open flea market
Dollars folding
Shoulders holding
Hands lifting
Soul shifting
Grocery-carted
Damaged & undamaged goods
Microwaves
Televisions
Air conditioners
In the summertime
Retailers
Wholesalers
Hustlers
Customers
Everybody in their own classified job.
Looking out for the cops

While

Coping

Dealing/wheeling

Copping/cropping

With the drug of choice

With no remorse

In the Big D.

☠

Around the curves of the boulevard

One hundred yard dash

Wife-beater-wearing blood chased by the police

By foot

Coffee & donut eating policeman gave up.

☠

Yo'! What up doe?

Yae-o $ rocks out here

☠

Lost it

&

Want it back

☠

Drugged me & got me for 2 grand / seen him 2 years later thought I was

Gonna kill him

☠

If there's drugs

There's always a head

That will climb a pole

To cut yo cable/gas/internet/light/water on

☠

The House
Don't get it twisted
The House
U just smoke there
Don't cop
Can't get raided
I said it
Only take u where
Go smoke it there

☠

That's how u hit & run
Make a tax-free million
&
Leave the hood
Faraway into the country

☠

Smell like burnt plastic

☠

To keep blow fresh
Wrap it 4 sale with catered bubble gum wrap or aluminum foil

☠

Homemade pipes. Use aluminum foil & a pencil for shape & a small
coil
Of chore boy so u can't lose it (the dope) dope!

☠

No disability can't stop the effect of the drug liability
Double deuce deaf dumb consumers

Baby boomers
Sign language for the goon zoom
☠
Super soak coke from coast to coast
No joke
Automatic remote
When she smoked
She smoked
When he smoked
He smoked
Witness to no more tokes
I have spoke about their smoke.
☠

Gird your mind
Not absurd
Pure Divine
☠

Gotta a slack kid
Mid 80's Kools was the thang
Now…
☠

Homeless 4
14 years
Now clean 4
4 years
Less tears
No fears
I hears

Cheers

☠

Pop the trunk & someone's inside. Corpse of course

☠

Ran into & ran up

☠

Surf on my turf / identified AK – 47 bullets is your curse

☠

Shoddy out slum shoppers for dope

☠

Doing the Debo like Fridays

☠

Fine asinine

Selective invective

Bold directive

Corrective

☠

Obama major like Dr. Martin Luther King

My Friend Let's Do It Again

Recycle the high

Conserve your nerves

Blow the inhaled white smoke exhaled in a knotted ballon

To resume & consume

Later / Fatal

Or

Blow the white smoke in a miracle-whip jar with a seal for a 2nd thrill

To close kill

Gases of moisture transforms to unholy ghost powders

Put alcohol / liquor /Don Q / 151 rum in the jar afar

Shake it up

Residue turns brown

Pour it on a flame-retardant glass mirror

Set a fire flicker on the liquor

Dry it to retry it

Scrape with a razor blade under the window shade

Ready to smoke again the same sin

Smoke slow you got more / High / Can't Deny / No Lie

Jail Tales

Male & Female
With no bail
Limited mail
Similar to Hell
With no smoke or fire
Yell & Tell
Open heaven over your life
Just a matter of TIME…
Don't pass GO
Don't collect 2 hundred doll'ahs
Holla!

☠

King culprit
King baby
At gunpoint
Damned damp tramp stamp
Tattooed taboos in rainbow living colors
THIEF
I FUCKED UP
On yo face
2 band-aid cover-up
Branded for the rest of yo natural born life
Got stuck on stupid
2 months later

B & E in the burbs
Took the keys
ONSTAR
3 blocks later
Now jail is his thang
Life party, hot waterbug body & no toddy
5 feet fo'
Light-skinned
Hip roll
Beginning of the BANG!
Jackson
God is there
10 years
Everywhere
☠
No pearl up the purps
☠
No bail menu
Items few
Crushed ramen noodles/ cheese sauce / cookies in a bag
&
Run it under hot water
Well balanced meal with a seal
Starch / Protein / Carbohydrate
With no debate
Or
Frozen p.b. & j. sandwiches & a wish
☠

Get up and can't go 2 da stoe

Or the gas station

☠

Bustin' a scripts of oxy-cotton & Vicodin for 2 c-notes & got busted

Should'a got 5 & did time

More than the 1st sin / worse force / designated curse

☠

5*11*5

Breakfast by 5

Lunch by 11

Dinner at 5

Miss them numbers

You be out

&

Be mad

Mystery meat, beans, goulash,

Pinkish green hot dogs & potato sticks

Everything u eat there

Mandatory gourmet

U got to bless it

A so true tale about the jail cell

☠

Last bag ended with a swisher & no ecstasy

☠

Raided & got 5 thou out the safe

☠

Negotiating 10 – 15 years

☠

Remember Joseph

☠

Before the jail cell
Police tale
I smell weed
Get the dogs to bite U

☠

A point about the joint
Gainfully employed
18 cents a' hour

☠

Fentanyl
Lethal dose cut with heroin killed hundred in the D
Dealer who dealt
20 YEARS

☠

Blood Is Red

Drop a dime

Crime doing time

Black girl, black girl your blood in red

Under lockdown 24/7 with a bunk bed / no dominoes / no cards / no

soul music / cup of coffee is gold / pay phone talking is a precious

luxury / no toothpaste & no toothbrush

Drop a dime

Crime doing time

White girl, white girl your blood is red

Not under lockdown 24/7 with a bunk bed / playing dominoes / playing

cards / listening to honky-tonk music / sipping java & joe / chatting on

the pay phone / toothpaste & toothbrush

Black girl / White girl

The blood is red

Slow yo role / funnel the tunnel / communicate thru the toilet bowl

camole hole / water so low / words flow / drown free / men on top /

women on the bottom

Drop a dime

Crime doing time

A black girl, a black girl her blood in red

Under 18 / under ecstasy / jail cell mate / 140 days then court date / no

release / her momma died though / gave me complimentary toothpaste

& toothbrush

Got out

Where's my eleven bucks?

In patrol's safekeeping

No cigarettes / no nick / no pepsi / no coffee. What's up?

My Blood Is Red

☠

My eyez see…

Finale

Repent That Sin
Invite Him In & New Begin

From solid ground
Before the trump sound
Potential bound
Time to get down
Before it's too late to wipe the slate
Now is the time to renew your mind
In this era for the light in you to shine
God can use you to be His Voice
You have the freewill to decide – your choice
Sacrifice your self-desires - whatever they may be
Take Jesus for hire / do his Word / heavenly learning tree
In the midst of your problems
Help from God will solve them
Know that the Holy Spirit of God is around you
Wisdom for his chosen few
God will equip you
Comfort or danger zone
You can't do it alone

Conquer that ungodly urge
Time to ascend & Holy Trinity surge

Mucked it up

Smoked it up

Money splurge

Time to purge

Instead of the crack vial

Give God a dial

On the surface

Get on with your ordained purpose

Resist exist

Kill the spirit of fear & dread

Enough said

In the manuscript

It's written - be dead

Steal, kill & destroy / crack isn't a toy

Drug abuse & misuse

There's no excuse for the obtuse abuse

It's cheaper to stay with the Lord today

More at stake when you disobey

Pretty please relate to what I say

Homestead ahead

Heavenly led

By Jesus stripes you're healed

Regardless of high or low you may feel

A hip tip to the fellowship

Lamb's Book of Life membership

When faith, prayer, praise, worship & the Word in sight

Spiritual maturity is in flight

What a blanket of surety

Almighty wings of emotional security
Repent that sin
Invite Him in & new begin
Prayer changes uncontrollable things
The just shall walk by faith
I sing
The impossible is possible
Sing a new song
Testimony upon testimony
Nothing is phony
What I write is true
God's perfect will is available to you
No need to be down in the dumps & blue
Dismiss that profane behavior
You have blessed & perfect Savior
Jesus is a curse killer & healer
God is married to the back slider
Waiting for you to turn around
Hurry up, hear the sound
As a child, I have been taught to exalt
Undefeated victory is the score
Jesus is at the door
Time for no more
Open up the DOOR!
Soar!
Roar!
Conquer!
Splendor & Glory tells the story

Invite Him In & New Begin
In Jesus Name, Amen
I Send / The End!